Dor

Rise Up!

24 Ways to Overcome Obstacles and Achieve your Destiny

GLENDA SENTELL JORDAN

Copyright © 2024 Glenda Sentell Jordan

ALL RIGHTS RESERVED. No part of this book or its associated ancillary materials may be reproduced or transmitted in any form or by any means, electronic or mechanical, including photocopying, recording, or by any informational storage or retrieval system without permission from the publisher.

DISCLAIMER AND/OR LEGAL NOTICES
While all attempts have been made to verify information provided in this book and its ancillary materials, neither the author nor publisher assumes any responsibility for errors, inaccuracies or omissions and is not responsible for any financial loss by customers in any manner. Any slights of people or organizations are unintentional. If advice concerning legal, financial, accounting or related matters is needed, the services of a qualified professional should be sought. This book and its associated ancillary materials, including verbal and written training, is not intended for use as a source of legal, financial or accounting advice. You should be aware of the various laws governing business transactions or other business practices in your particular geographic location.

The author has made every effort to ensure the accuracy of the information within this book was correct at time of publication. The author does not assume and hereby disclaims any liability to any party for any loss, damage, or disruption caused by errors or omissions, whether such errors or omissions result from accident, negligence, or any other cause.

Any examples, stories, references or case studies are for illustrative purposes only and should not be interpreted as testimonies and/or examples of what readers and/or consumers can expect. Any statements, strategies, concepts, techniques, exercises and ideas in this information, materials and/or seminar training offered are simply opinion or experience, and thus should not be misinterpreted as promises.

Testimonials

"It has been rewarding to watch Glenda's posture and walk improve, as I have supported her with chiropractic adjustments through her journey. She has also been a blessing by sharing her experiences with us at our ministry where we teach about how Jesus already provided for our healing (according to I Peter 2:24)."

—**Dr. Gary Johns,** Healing in the House
healinginhouse@gmail.com

"I first met Glenda in 2009. She wanted to minimize her limp on videos where she would be dancing with her son on his wedding day in four weeks. I performed cold laser protocols, over the next four weeks ending with lasering her while dancing with her basically lasering in peak performance of a box step. We reconnected in early 2023. Glenda stood up and walked across the room, I was moved to tears, as the difference in her walk was breathtaking. When I first met Glenda, her passion in her relationship with Christ was infectious. Then to have seen her all those years later, seeing what her level of faith in Christ had created in her level of well-being was inspirational. The results obtained from implementing the actions Glenda describes in her book are truly remarkable."

– **Linda Mitchell-Vargo,** ND, RDH

"It is with the greatest pleasure that I endorse Glenda's book wholeheartedly. I had the pleasure of meeting Glenda while providing thermographic imaging for her to assess the physiologic state of her body. What I saw on screen and read in her Polio history didn't correlate with the vibrant, positive woman with whom I was interacting. Glenda "walks the walk" she professes. Not only is that evident in her persona, but also in measurable science. Due to her desire and diligence to make positive changes in her health, she did. The evidence of increased circulation and reduced inflammation were evident on a subsequent thermographic examination. All things are indeed possible by faith, and she exemplifies that faith in such an easily relatable and unpretentious way. I'm thankful she decided to listen to friends and Spirit to share her faith walk now rather than wait. Thank you, Glenda and may God's grace and healing continue to be evident in your life."

  –Nina Rea, BCTT

Patsy and I have watched Glenda grow in Faith in God's Word for over 23 years. She walks by Faith and not by Sight. She knows that things seen are temporary, but Gods Word is Eternal. Her Diligence in confessing God's Word is bringing her Great Rewards of His Promises.

  –Pastors Bryan and Patsy White

Motivate and Inspire Others!

"Share This Book"

Retail $21.95

Special Quantity Discounts

5-20 Books	$18.95
21-99 Books	$15.95
100-499 Books	$11.95
500-999 Books	$9.95
1,000+ Books	$6.95

To Place an Order Contact:

DontGiveUpRiseUpBook@gmail.com

The Ideal Professional Speaker For Your Next Event!

Any organization that wants to develop people to become "extraordinary" needs to hire Glenda for a keynote and/or workshop training!

To Contact or Book Glenda to Speak:

DontGiveUpRiseUpBook@gmail.com

I dedicate this book to my sons and their families:

Mark and Therese Rinehart

Matthew and Allison Rinehart and family
(Marie, Lena, Silas, Everett, and Arthur)

You all give my life meaning, and without you, I would not be the person I am today. I love you dearly!

An African proverb says that it takes a village to raise a child. I sincerely appreciate the many people who have actively supported me on this journey. You are the village that helped me to rise up.

Royal and Barbara Clevenger

Kathy Elzey

Dr. Steve Gonian

Wendy Hood

Dr. Gary and Lou Ann Johns

Mira Keeley

Dr. Li Liu, O.M.D., L. Ac

Dr. Yuxian Annie Liu, L. Ac

Linda Mitchell-Vargo, ND, RDH

Nina Rea, Certified Thermographic Technician

Shyamala Strack, OTR/L, CST-D

Pastors Bryan and Patsy White

Contents

Begin and end the day with your power source. 1

Kindle the god-given desire to grow. 7

Realign your life to reflect each concept and new revelation learned. 11

Allow the dreams buried inside of you to be identified. 15

See what you want clearly so you can achieve it. 19

Feed what you want to grow. 23

Chart the direction of your life with the end in mind. 27

Monitor your thoughts throughout the day. 31

Speak what you want in your life. 35

Read your emotions and respond to balance your life. 39

Make the decision to eradicate fear and every other negative spirit. 43

Develop a strategy for your life. 47

Track your progress daily 51

Embrace change. 55

Spend time with the people that you would like to become. 59

Renew your mind daily. 63

Identify mentors and remain coachable. 67

Maintain a nutritious diet. 71

Exercise regularly. 75

Listen to the perspective of others around you. 79

Provide more value than you
receive everywhere you go. 83

Have an attitude of gratitude. 87

Keep your momentum going.. 91

Invest your life well. 95

Cultivating my personal relationship with god....................... 99

The Story Behind This Book

I contracted polio when I was six months old before any polio vaccine was available. The virus attacked the left side of my brain, resulting in paralysis on the right side of my body. The doctors told my parents that I would never walk correctly. The medical professionals predicted my right leg would be three inches shorter than my left, I would eventually need the tendon on my right ankle cut, and I would drag my right leg as I walked with braces and crutches. My mom quickly decided that was not what God intended for my life. She did not understand anything about supernatural healing, but she understood practical steps to keep my muscles alive. Polio was the dreaded disease of the day, and machines in certain medical facilities could be rented to reduce muscle atrophy. My parents did not have the money to use these machines daily, and the waiting list to use the machines would have delayed frequent use anyway. Mom watched how the machines worked my leg, and she dedicated five hours a day every day to exercising my leg and arm in the same way. I was able to walk without a leg brace by the age of six. I walked with a small limp, but I walked!

As time passed, my back did not grow properly because of the limp. When I was standing as if I were facing the 12:00 o'clock position, X-rays later revealed that my hip was facing 11:00 o'clock. When I was standing "straight", my left shoulder was higher than my right, and my spine curved around to keep everything connected. As a result, painful arthritis and bone spurs developed. The area of my body that reflected the most damage was the outside calf of my right leg. By the time I was 65, the muscle along the outside calf of my right leg had deteriorated and the bone was noticeable to the touch. As a child, I learned that a primary way to receive instruction from God was through the Bible. I had read that He promised total restoration and healing through His Word. About 12 years ago, after much prayer I decided to believe Him and began to meditate on relevant passages of scripture.

A separate complication I dealt with is known as post-polio syndrome, which is a condition that can cause muscle weakness and atrophy decades after recovering from the initial poliovirus infection. In my case, I was losing strength in my left hand and could no longer snap my fingers. I rely on that hand more than an average left-handed person. I contacted a friend who performed an alternative health method, known as EDS (Electro-Dermal Stress) analysis. EDS analysis is based on a Chinese medical concept that energy flows through the acupuncture meridians of the body. The technique measures balance and imbalance found in the organs, glands, and/or systems. The analysis also identifies which nutritional or homeopathic remedies, along with exact potencies, will bring the body into energy balance. The oral tinctures that my friend recommended restored full movement in my hand within a matter of weeks. Those symptoms occurred five years ago and have never returned. At that time, I was meditating on scripture about God's promises of healing and also exercising daily. However, progress in restoring the atrophy of the muscles impacted by the original infection was slow.

This same friend, who became my mentor, recommended a chiropractor who was willing to assess my situation. Over the years, I had many discussions with other medical professionals, who felt restoration of my muscle tissue was not possible. I was eager to try a reference from this friend for chiropractic care. The chiropractor performed a detailed examination and took X-rays. He believed that I could rebuild 40% of my right calf muscle. The chiropractor recommended that I see his personal trainer, and I began an exercise program three times a week. I also received chiropractic adjustments with each visit. The exercises were challenging, and I tired easily. At that time, certain muscles would move, but I could not feel them moving without touching my leg with my hand. I began to wear yoga pants, as the tightness of the fabric allowed me to feel the muscles moving more easily. Other muscles would not engage to allow the desired movements, which was very frustrating. During exercise, I would frequently throw my back and hips out of alignment because the muscles in my leg and core were so weak. The trainer would often hold my foot or leg in place so that the correct muscles would be exercised. After exercising the pain was often intense. The doctor said the pain I felt was to be expected because I was recalibrating my spine and hips, and all my muscles were moving differently. I did progress and chiropractic visits were gradually reduced. I found a trainer at a local gym to assist with my exercise regime. However, the year was 2020, and after locating a trainer with the right background for me, all the gyms closed due to COVID. The chiropractor was also released from the clinic where he worked and the clinic eventually closed.

During 2020, I continued my meditation and exercise routine. One day, as I prayed about how to locate the support that I needed, I thought about an instructor for a class I took at church–her face kept coming into my mind. Her name was Wendy Hood and I knew that she did kickboxing. She knew who I was from the class, and we had previously traded phone numbers. After seeing Wendy's face multiple times during my quiet time, I gave her a call. Wendy was a health coach. She was not familiar with polio, but she listened and took lots of notes. She reviewed the information from the chiropractor's trainer and agreed to work with me twice a week. I continued to work with Wendy through that summer.

My body strength continued to improve, and so did my belief in God's Word. If I believed that the price for my total health was paid for on a cross 2,000 years ago, then I needed to stop focusing my recovery on only the atrophied muscles. I needed to behave as if my body was already restored. I discussed this new revelation with Wendy. By now, I knew she was a martial arts black belt. So, when she suggested martial arts as the best way to strengthen all the muscles in my body and develop the balance that I never had, I agreed to try it. Our training sessions became martial arts lessons.

Fast forward to today. I have a green belt in martial arts, the fourth of 10 belts in Song Moo Do Martial Arts. My body strength continues to improve. I continue to study healthy living and have taken other actions to improve my overall health as well. The arthritis in my right hand has gone away. I have never had updated X-rays of my back, but it is now straight, and all the pain is gone.

Three different women, who knew me before this journey started, have been brought to tears watching me exercise or walk. Many other friends have communicated their amazement. I knew I wanted to document my story at some point in the future. However, two separate people in ministry, who do not know each other, have recently asked me to mentor them. Both observed my passion for life and drive to reach my destiny. Both want the same for their lives and ministries. I originally felt that I needed to attain a black belt or see my health and wellness business grow before people would benefit from my new perspective. However, others are already motivated by what they see in me and suggested that I write a book, so I decided to share these tips that I regularly practice now.

1

Begin and end the day with your power source.

Two of the most important times of the day are the very beginning when we wake up and the very end, right before we close our eyes. We can plan our focus at the beginning of the day and we can quiet our minds at the end of the day.

The human spirit can be like a car battery that is losing power. A source that is bigger and more powerful is needed to reenergize it. Sometimes people are influenced by things out in the world and receive a temporary boost of energy—a jump-start. Attending a meeting, getting involved in a cause, or becoming excited about an activity can boost their energy. This boost may influence them to donate money or call their senator to express their opinion but, after a week or two, they are no longer taking any action for that same cause because they were motivated by something on the outside. No internal drive existed; no power source was engaged. A jump-start was needed before any action could be taken. Without a good battery, power cannot be retained.

When you look back in history, many whose names are remembered through time seemed to have an inexhaustible battery, a power source greater than themselves. Examples include Joan of Arc, Martin Luther King, and Mother Teresa. These people had a cause they believed in that was much bigger than themselves. These leaders were plugged into that cause, or power source, and driven by their beliefs. They did not need a jump-start. When problems came, they looked for ways to deal with the barriers. Overcoming the obstacles was part of what they were called to do.

For me, my power source is the God of Abraham, Isaac, and Jacob. Every morning when I wake up, I welcome Elohim (Father, Son, and Holy Spirit) into my day, into my life, and into my thoughts. And then I listen. Sometimes a song will cross my mind that I had not thought of in years, and I will start singing a song of praise. Sometimes I speak what I hear inside me, which could be scripture verses or specific statements. I thank God repeatedly for how valuable He is, what He has done in my life, what He is doing in my life, and the protection He provides. The thoughts just well up inside of me. During these conversations, I get my direction for the day.

In the same way, I close out the day by thanking God for what He has done for me. I review my day by thinking about things that maybe I could have done differently, or that I can do better tomorrow. Connecting to our power source is critical to our success, as we receive energy to expend throughout the day and direction on how to allocate our time during the day. The energy improves our attitude, and the intentional allocation of time allows us to be more satisfied with our daily accomplishments.

Note: If you currently do not have an active communication with God as I have just described and desire to have one, please see "Cultivating my personal relationship with God" in the Conclusion.

2

Kindle the God-given desire to grow.

Growth is an integral principle of life. Imagine a seed in the ground. That seed grows into a plant and produces other seeds. The new seeds grow into more plants that produce more seeds. The same thing happens with animal and insect life. Everything grows, everything expands. As human beings, we should grow and expand also. Many of us get married and have children and that is certainly one way to expand. We can also expand ourselves, our inner being, to continue providing more and more blessings and impact others in a positive way.

In nature, when growth and development stop, we recognize it as a problem. In the case of a tree that no longer produces leaves, we know the roots are not good and we cut it down. We know the presence of that tree represents danger when a storm comes because the tree will not have the strength to stand. The same can happen with humans. As we go through life and experience struggles and other traumas, we may become closed off and no longer able to produce the blessings that God desires us to generate.

The key to growth is planting the right information in the heart. The heart is the soil of the soul. Whatever we allow to enter our eyes and ears can be implanted in our hearts and grow. For me, reading and meditating on the Word of God each day is essential. During my morning time with the Lord, I read or listen to five chapters of the Bible, talking with God and asking Him questions as I read. The more I read and study, the clearer and more actionable the concepts become. I also spend on average 30 minutes a day reading other books to sharpen my skills on various subjects. Books such as *"How to Win Friends & Influence People"* by *Dale Carnegie*, *"The Compound Effect"* by *Darren Hardy*, and *"Grit"* by *Angela Duckworth* provide modern-day examples of how the principles in God's Word work.

We can rekindle the desire to grow by reading and learning God's Word. Regardless of our age or circumstances, there are always things we can do, always things we can learn, and always new ways to impact the world in a positive manner. We need to understand that growth and development are essential to life. Strive to make sure that this month you have grown over last month. Do something each day to grow as an individual.

3

Realign your life to reflect each concept and new revelation learned.

As I study the Word and as I talk with God, scriptures will sometimes jump off the page. I'll see something that I need to do differently, or I'll understand a deeper meaning than I previously had. For example, Scripture says not to be in debt; to owe no man anything but love. After reading that passage many years ago, I made a conscious decision to pay off my credit cards each month. God was telling me not to have debt if I wanted an optimal life. While getting out of debt may take time, pressing toward that goal is a decision that can be made.

We need to consecrate ourselves to each new insight. We will then be open to receiving a new revelation. Like any good coach, often God will not tell us anything else until we have already done what He last told us.

Similarly, we must implement the laws of the kingdom of God as soon as we identify them. Within the scriptures, there are spiritual laws. A lot of scripture is based on sowing the seeds and harvesting the fruit. The common saying is that you reap what you sow or what goes around comes around. That is a description of seed time and harvest as referenced throughout the scriptures. Spiritual laws are at work, whether we understand them or not. For example, if we give more value than what we are receiving in an activity or business transaction, then we will be blessed in that activity or business.

If we speak only positive things and think only positive thoughts, then we are going to draw positive things back to us. If we think negatively, the law of attraction is going to bring negative things to us. These spiritual laws are described in scriptures such as the "Sermon on the Mount" in the New Testament (Matthew 5-7). Jesus said, "Seek ye first the kingdom of God, and all these things shall be added unto you." He didn't say seek God. Jesus said to seek the *kingdom* of God. He was saying to seek to understand how God operates. When we understand how God has designed His kingdom, and operate within those precepts, then everything else will be added unto us.

From my perspective, reading and studying the scriptures without applying the concepts outlined within is like reading the instructions for assembling a desk but never putting the furniture together. I don't want to simply discuss the desk with a group of friends or describe the benefits of the desk to others. I am reading the instructions as a prerequisite to using the desk. Action is needed to bring benefit in every area of life. In my case, when I believed I had total restoration, I stopped rehabilitating only the muscles that atrophied or were damaged from polio. I began taking martial arts lessons because healthy people exercise their entire body.

4

Allow the dreams buried inside of you to be identified.

As children, we have dreams of who we want to be. We imagine ourselves having certain careers or having different adventures. Sometimes they do not seem necessarily practical things for real life. Maybe we want to be a superhero with a cape or a dinosaur that roams the plains. As we grow up, some of these dreams evolve into real and vivid things that we can attain. However, we can talk ourselves out of these dreams because they do not seem practical enough. We cannot see a way to accomplish the desires we had as a child.

If we eat soup with a knife, we can get some of the liquid; however, a spoon was specifically made for scooping up soup and a knife was made to cut solid foods. Therefore, we should use a spoon. If we are in the wrong place or doing the wrong thing, we are not going to be effective in life or satisfied with the outcome.

God's Word tells us that He has a destiny for each of us. He created each of us to do certain things. Deep inside of us is the desire to do what we are designed to do.

As I thought about this concept for myself, I knew that developing and motivating others was a part of God's plan for me. This was reinforced by people commenting on how well I could explain ideas, even as a young child. As an adult, this was further reinforced by feedback from my corporate bosses praising my ability to motivate my team to accomplish specific goals.

The dream will be different for each of us. We can spend time thinking about what it is that we really want to do and work with our imagination to develop our path. True fulfillment will come when we do what we were created to do. The caped superhero becomes a law officer or firefighter. The roaming dinosaur becomes an archaeologist or specifically a paleontologist. Getting a clearer vision of the dreams that live within you can help move you forward today.

5

*See what you want clearly
so you can achieve it.*

People say, "I'll believe it when I see it." People of faith often say that you cannot see it until you believe it; you must use faith. In a way, we do have to see it to receive it. If people are sick and are expecting God to supernaturally heal them, they must first see themselves as a healthy person. They must see themselves well in their mind's eye, the inner self, what we might call the imagination.

We must see ourselves in abundance if our goal is to be financially successful. We must act on what Jesus said in Mark 11:23b, which is that if a person "does not doubt in his heart, but believes that what he says will come to pass, he will have whatever he says." We need to say what we want, not describe what we are lacking. That does not mean that we are immediately wealthy or that the symptoms of whatever illness we experience will go away instantly. It does mean that we can see ourselves how we really are spiritually. The desired condition will manifest over time only when we have a clear picture.

When developers build physical structures, they have an architect create a blueprint first. Architectural designs are very detailed, sometimes with 3D video displays of how the building will look when completed. The developer clearly understands the details before breaking ground. The same can be true of our dreams and what we want to achieve. We must conceive, design, and nurture the vision inside of us to bring it into reality.

In my case, I see myself performing martial arts moves flawlessly all during the day, even when I am not practicing. I envision the right side of my body having the same strength as my left. As I draft this book, I am using all five fingers on my right hand, which I could not have done several years ago. I conceived it. I designed it. It is up to me to bring it into reality by taking action on my belief in God's promises and the process He designed for us to succeed..

6

Feed what you want to grow.

Whatever we feed is what will grow around us. Imagine a garden where only certain crops are fed and tended. The nutrients, water, etc. that are right for those particular plants are provided. Those plants will flourish. However, the other plants in the garden that have been neglected will be overgrown with weeds or suffer from pest infestation and most likely not grow to full maturity. Left on their own, they cannot grow. We must take the necessary actions if we want those plants to grow.

We grow our dreams in the same manner. We can decide who we want to be and what we want to do. We have our dream and a clear vision of how we want it to lay out. Now we must tend to it and feed it the proper nutrients, the thoughts that will help us achieve our goal.

In my case, I am restoring my whole body from polio and I am using martial arts as a vehicle to build back the strength in my muscles. I must see myself executing the martial arts forms correctly. While writing this book, I can already feel that the tendons in my foot are now working more effectively even though medical professionals said that could not happen. I can now move my right foot correctly up and down. I cannot yet move that foot from side to side. However, in my mind, I see my foot moving in all directions smoothly while I am doing the martial arts forms. I see the forms the way they are supposed to look. My body will conform to what I see because that is how God made me, and I understand that is how God made all of us. When we see it, we focus and feed ourselves on it, then we will obtain what we see.

7

Chart the direction of your life with the end in mind.

Imagine planning a trip. We think about where we want to end up and when we want to be there. We select a mode of travel—plane, bus, train, or auto. We determine what is the best way to reach our destination, including the cost and time required. Then we set things in motion.

Along the way, there can be detours or obstacles depending on the mode and route we choose. If I decide to drive from Atlanta to Dallas, at some point I will come to an intersection. At this intersection, I see a road to the right is newly paved and in better shape than the road directly in front of me. I could take that newer road because it looks like an easy and fun ride. However, the smooth road leads to Canada, which is a great place, but my goal is Texas. Heading toward Canada is not going to get me to my destination. At best I am going to lose a lot of time. I will save that trip for another adventure.

Once we decide on our destination or our goal, then we need to chart our journey. A clear understanding of our destination will enable us to say yes to certain opportunities and no to others. A lot of choices may present themselves along the way, but we must stay focused on those things that will help us achieve our goals and say no to other activities that might take us in the wrong direction.

8

Monitor your thoughts throughout the day.

In Philippians 4:8-9, Paul tells us we should think about the things that are true, pure and good. Whatever we have learned from the scripture, we should put into practice.

Monitoring what one thinks is hard work and takes practice. I must do it every day to keep myself on track for my goals. When I am unable to do an exercise the way I think I should be able to do it, if the thought crosses my mind that *"I am never going to be able to do this,"* I must immediately say to myself *"I forget that thought".* Then I tell myself to remember that two months ago, I could not do what I am doing now. I may not be able to stand up without my hands after kneeling on one knee; however, now I can get down on one knee. I will eventually be able to get up. I must constantly practice monitoring my thoughts and focusing on what is true, pure, and good to ensure that I am thinking the thoughts that will keep me headed in the direction I want to go.

9

Speak what you want in your life.

Our words are also very powerful. The book of Proverbs, written by Solomon, acclaimed to be the wisest man in the world, states that death and life are in the power of the tongue and that they that love it will eat the fruit thereof. Speaking what we want is essential to obtaining our desires. We should not talk about what we are experiencing if our current reality is not what we want.

When God created the earth, the scripture doesn't record Him as saying, "Wow, it is dark out here!" In Genesis 1:3, it is written that God said, "Let there be light: and there was light." The concept of speaking the desired outcome is clear throughout the scriptures.

In Genesis 17:5, God changed Abram's name to Abraham, because He "had made" Abraham a father of many nations. Abraham's only son was Ishmael at that point in time. In I Kings 17:40-47, David announced that he would cut Goliath's head off that very day, even though he did not have a sword in his possession. In Mark 5:35-42, Jesus said that the child was not dead. He stated she was sleeping and proceeded to call her back from the dead. Each person was speaking into existence the desired outcome because they understood the power that their words created.

I have personal experience with saying what I want. I have had several experiences in my business, but the most dramatic examples are related to my health. Even though the restoration in my body from polio has been progressive, a few years ago the restoration of my eyesight was more immediate. One morning four years ago, while I was getting ready to go to the optometrist, I was thinking about how I was increasingly tired of having to reach for glasses to read anything. I had been wearing glasses since the fifth grade. The vision tests reflected near-sightedness and astigmatism. As I aged, I also became far-sighted. Several of the scripture verses I had been meditating on at that time for restoration from polio included healing the blind as well as the lame. I examined my belief level that morning and said out loud in my bedroom that I would only need to wear eyeglasses part-time. I had been wearing glasses or contacts full-time for over 55 years. I walked out of the optometrist's office later that morning with a prescription for a small vision correction. The doctor's recommendation was to wear the glasses if my eyes grew tired. I have not had a need to wear glasses since then.

10

Read your emotions and respond to balance your life.

Emotions can be indicator lights for what is happening inside our minds and bodies. They are valid and need to be addressed. We should not deny what we are feeling. Positive emotions can increase life and health; however, living in negative emotions can hinder our growth and literally make us sick.

Some "feelings" or emotions can be spiritual in nature, such as fear. Our response to fear can be anger or anxiety. We need to recognize what is happening in our minds and deal with the thoughts coming from those emotions.

My personal remedy for feeling anxiety is to meditate on Psalm 23. In that passage, David tells us that God is always with us and will always provide for us; therefore, no reason to be anxious exists.

Sometimes anger can be redirected into a positive action. For example, an emotion of anger while watching a movie about human trafficking could be channeled into taking action to help prevent such a crime from happening.

The appropriate remedy for each emotion depends on the thoughts that created the emotion or the emotion that created the thoughts. Understanding the thoughts that create positive emotions assists us in duplicating the process. Reading the passage in Psalm 23 gives me good hopeful thoughts and alleviates my anxiety. Changing our thoughts will change our emotions.

11

Make the decision to eradicate fear and every other negative spirit.

A direct output of reading your emotions is gaining the ability to make a quality decision before any negative emotion is on your horizon. You can decide not to tolerate fear or any related byproduct. The scriptures tell us repeatedly not to fear, which means fear is a choice we make. The Bible also states in I John 4:18 that perfect love will cast out all fear. Given that fear is a choice, you can simply engage your faith and say, "I will not fear." You must not envy or take offense at anything. Negative reactions only damage you, not the other person that you may have felt is generating the obstacle for you.

My grandchildren will often say that their sibling made them do something or made them feel angry. No outside influence or person "makes" us do or feel anything. We decide how we respond. We need to put away all envy, strife, and offense. Choose love and the byproducts of love in every situation. Our bodies were made to flourish with love, which is agape in Greek, and it is best defined in I Corinthians 13 of the New Testament. To the extent that we do not dwell in that love walk, we cannot function as a whole and healthy human being. We must decide how to respond before any incidents come our way. Then when adversity strikes, our decision has already been made, and we only need to act accordingly.

In my life, meditating on I Corinthians 13 and other readings on the love walk is my response to keeping myself focused on being positive regardless of my current circumstances.

12

Develop a strategy for your life.

Once we have a goal and direction, we are ready to create a strategy to achieve our goals. In my case, I chose prayer and relied on my unwavering faith in God, which led to finding a trainer willing to help me with regular exercise. I also learned to advocate for myself with medical professionals.

I developed a strategy with my trainer to move my body into a pre-diseased condition with the goal of complete restoration. Establishing the proper mindset (as discussed later in section 16) is a prerequisite of a successful outcome. As I move through this process, I can attest to how I have received help in a practical and dramatic way from the Lord. Many people would think that after 70 years, the human body could not be restored, but I know differently.

13

Track your progress daily.

A daily review of what we have accomplished can help us stay on track. If a day does not yield the results we want, we can correct our activities the next day. We need to avoid making excuses by focusing on our intentions. If we examine our results, we are more likely to achieve our desired outcomes.

I have goals for exercising a certain amount of time every day for six days a week. I change my focus each week based on the feedback I receive from my martial arts instructor. I review my progress daily, and in the evening as I go to bed, I evaluate what I have done. If I did not accomplish what I wanted, I rethink the plan for the next day.

We use similar methods to keep track of goals in our businesses. We can track the number of contacts we make each day and the number of meetings we have so that we can evaluate our progress.

Part of my business/life strategy is to develop wealth so that I can distribute it to the causes that I am passionate about, which include restoring the kingdom of God throughout the world. For every goal I have, I monitor my progress.

14

Embrace change.

If we want growth in our lives, we must allow for change. Growth leads to change. We cannot resist change; we must look at it as a good thing. Change is always going to occur. If we are always growing, change will be a constant in our lives. Change will result in prioritizing relationships with people we did not previously have, going places we have not gone, and reading different materials than we have read before.

As we allow ourselves to grow and change, we see that this is an ongoing process, and we can embrace it. You may have heard, "If you always do what you have always done, then you will always get the same results you have always gotten." If we want something different from what we have, we must do something different going forward. Every day, I must be prepared to make changes in my life so I can reach the goals that I have set for myself. I open my mind and accept change. If I am not changing, I am not growing.

15

Spend time with the people that you would like to become.

My mother used to say that birds of a feather flock together. We are inevitably influenced by the people in our lives. Those individuals who have achieved certain goals and know where the obstacles are guide others through their journey. For some, helping people and assisting them to achieve their goals is part of their personal vison. We eventually become like the voices we listen to—the people we let into our inner circle.

We can also choose to spend time listening to and reading books by individuals who have experienced healing and restoration in their personal lives, as well as others who have contacted them for support. I listen to various podcasts during the week from leaders in the medical profession who have chosen holistic methods of healing. I do not know most of the individuals personally; however, through modern technology, I have spent more time learning from their materials than I could have if I were meeting with them in person.

If we are trying to succeed in business, then we want to find successful businesspeople to guide us. If we are hoping to succeed in ministry, then we want to select people who are achieving results in ministry. Sometimes, this requires us to move out of our comfort zones and meet new people. Sometimes this may require us to discontinue relationships with those who do not understand our motivation to move forward. My closest friends completely agree that my body can be totally restored, which supports my goals.

In my business, the associations I select are via a private mentorship group I joined several years ago. I was vetted and became a part of a team that is coaching me and providing materials for me to read. I attend meetings and listen to presentations with people who, primarily with a business focus, are developing themselves. The leaders of the group have already impacted thousands of lives individually and practice free enterprise around the world, which aligns with my business goals.

16

Renew your mind daily.

Setting a mental focus for each day is key to continued success. We need to focus and renew our minds because the general bent of our society, and much of what we experience in this fallen world, is negative. We need to ensure negative thoughts do not take up residence in our brains. We can feed our minds with the thoughts that will help us become the person that we want to be.

I generally work on my daily mindset as my day is just beginning. After I have finished my conversations and prayer with the Lord, I read or listen to several chapters of the Bible. I listen to something motivational for my business. I also read motivational materials for at least 15 minutes, something uplifting and positive, that will get me charged for the day.

17

Identify mentors and remain coachable.

In addition to associating with successful people, we can select individuals as mentors who will help us manage the details of our goals. The mentors we select can help keep us accountable to ourselves. Mentors who have achieved what we want to achieve are a vital asset. If we interact with them regularly, they can provide objective feedback on the progress we are making in achieving our goals. With a mentor's insights, we can identify what changes are needed to accelerate our progress.

To benefit from mentors, we need to remain coachable. If we feel that God has called us to associate with and lean on mentors, then we need to be open to what they say. The purpose of creating these relationships is to listen to and learn from the people who have already achieved the goals we desire. Like climbing a mountain, if people are already way above us on the mountain, they can tell us where the pitfalls are. They can tell us where the loose rocks are. We need to be listening to our mentors and not doing our own thing. Professional athletes always have one or more coaches, no matter how talented they are. Even if we think that we know better, we need to humble ourselves and do what they tell us to do. They have already traveled that path and have better insight than we have. Plus, mentors are not emotionally involved in our problems or the barriers in our lives, so they can often see how to handle things more clearly.

18

Maintain a nutritious diet.

Maintaining a healthy diet becomes more and more challenging as our world deteriorates. The typical diet does not provide the nutrients needed for a healthy body. For example, cooking fruits and vegetables removes enzymes that help with digestion. To act on that, we can eat more raw fruits and vegetables.

Healthy people value the nutritional reserves in their bodies. A food not known for nutrients, such as a doughnut, would take from the reserves in our bodies. Eating unhealthy food robs the digestive enzymes, vitamins, and minerals from other parts of our bodies to get the non-nutritious food processed. Although we can get the sugar high from the doughnut and feel satisfied, we are taking reserves away from our bodies. As we get older and continue to eat non-nutritious foods, the less reserves we have. This is part of the reason that so many people have a lot of health issues as they get into their late 50s, 60s, and 70s. They did not maintain what God designed in the body. As a result, the immune system is weak, and the body cannot effectively fight off disease. In many instances, prescription drugs that have unhealthy chemicals are also hindering the body's ability to maintain wellness. Much can be achieved by understanding how enzymes, minerals, vitamins, and alkaline levels in our body assist in maintaining health. The physical body is key to being able to function, and we must take care of all aspects of our physical bodies.

I have taken action by recently deciding to eat one uncooked meal, like a salad, each day. I also take digestive enzyme supplements and purchase much of my food from local farmers, who harvested the crops that same week. Each person must evaluate what actions to take for themselves. However, believing that we can continually eat processed foods and foods grown in mineral-depleted soil without taking additional actions to support our body processes is naive.

19

Exercise regularly.

Our physical bodies are very important, and our bodies were designed to move. My physical body is a key element in everything that I do because my primary goal is to restore my body. Even if our goals are not physical in nature, our body secretes hormones and chemicals that impact our thoughts. The health of our bodies impacts everything we do and how we feel. Exercising several times a week can be very beneficial. Information about aerobic and strength exercises is available everywhere. We need to make sure our bodies stay in good working condition because we cannot accomplish what God has called us to do if our bodies do not function.

As mentioned earlier, I exercise six times a week, one hour on two days and at least 30 minutes on the remaining four days.

20

Listen to the perspective of others around you.

When we are going about our daily routine, we need to listen to where other people are so that we can be a blessing. For example, one of the cashiers in a grocery store I frequent got very sick, and another cashier told me about it. This information prompted me to intercede in prayer for that person. I also talked with her when she returned to work, explaining some of the things that I do to maintain my health. She sees me buying celery regularly, so we discussed the benefits of juicing celery. Whenever we interact with people, we need to be listening to them. We can then give back, addressing what they expressed that they need. If we are not in a situation where we can give advice, contribute financially, or in some other physical way, we can certainly pray for them. Pray that the Lord will provide for their immediate needs and send laborers to teach them how to access God's provision for themselves directly.

When I go anywhere during the day, I focus my thoughts on the people around me. I look for how I can help them, which often starts by listening to what their needs are in their daily lives.

21

Provide more value than you receive everywhere you go.

The principle of seed and harvest is activated when you give. We will receive because of what we give, although our reward may not be reaped from the person to whom we gave. When we provide more value than we receive, both we and the recipient are blessed. Providing value is a no-lose situation because we will eventually gain from the action in some way.

We can look for ways to provide more value as we interact with people. For example, I am a representative for health and wellness products, which will enhance my customers' lives and health. I also interact with the customers and regularly talk about how best to use the products. If what was purchased is not making a positive change in their lives, I will suggest a different product or strategy to remedy the concern. I provide extra value by following up with my clients to ensure they receive the desired outcomes.

I also share things that I do in my life as examples of actions others can take to make their lives better. My martial arts lessons are private in-home lessons, but I often invite other people to watch me test for the next belt by asking them to run the camera so that I can keep track of my improvement. I select people who are interested in the benefits of martial arts and could be potential clients for my coach. This helps them to see what martial arts is about, and I am also providing extra value to my coach in addition to what I pay her for the lessons.

22

Have an attitude of gratitude.

Gratitude is essential in everything we do. God instructs us in Psalm 100 to enter His gates with thanksgiving in our hearts and enter His courts with praise. Thanking God, thanking those around us, and being appreciative of everything that we have been given multiplies the blessings coming back to us. The more gratitude we have, the more we will be blessed, and the better we will feel. We will draw the positive things that we want by being thankful for what we already have.

I often thank my grandchildren for picking up their toys, and I tell them that I appreciate what they have done. That encouragement motivates them to pick up the toys next time. The younger grandchildren start helping because they see me honoring the older grandchildren. The concept works at every level of life with every person. Gratitude is essential to a successful life and a positive frame of mind.

23

Keep your momentum going.

When we start a journey and incorporate new things into our lives, circumstances can challenge our ability to create the good habits needed to accomplish our goals. We are often interrupted by family vacations or changes to our schedules. When we must change our routine for two weeks or even two days, it can be like starting over to re-engage. Momentum to build a positive spirit is going to increase each day that we accomplish the routine we select. People are going to be aware that we are going somewhere with our lives. If we take a long pause, the energy we have built up in ourselves will begin to evaporate little by little. Although schedules do change, if we were driving down a road and saw that the original path was blocked by construction, would we not take a detour to reach our desired destination? The same is true with our daily habits.

Sometimes I get up extra early to keep certain appointments. I then make a conscious decision to get up even earlier, so that I can pray and fellowship with God before my day starts. I might schedule another time to read that day. I may take a "detour" from my normal process, but I do not stop my routine. When I have stopped for some interruption in life circumstances, the day does not flow as well. And if my day is not the same, my attitude is not the same. If I stop for several days, I really lose ground. The journey is an everyday process for the rest of my life. I must maintain momentum if I want to achieve the maximum potential in my life.

24

Invest your life well.

How we spend our time and resources matters to every life we might influence along the way. In Matthew 25, Jesus tells the parable of a ruler who traveled to a far country that perfectly illustrates this point. Before the man left, he gave one servant five talents, another servant two talents, and a third servant received one talent, based on each person's ability. (A talent was a monetary measure, used in this case to signify something of value.) The first two individuals invested what they had been given and doubled their resources. Both individuals were told that they were good and faithful. The men kept the original gifts, the increase obtained, and received additional honors. The individuals did something with what they were given based on the abilities they possessed. The third person buried the gift until the owner returned. When giving an account for his actions, the third man said that the ruler was a harsh man and harvested where he had not sown. The man said that he buried the talent so he would not lose it. The ruler called the third person's bluff. He called the individual a wicked, which meant twisted thinking, and slothful (lazy) man. If he was concerned about losing the talent, he could have deposited it in the bank and earned interest.

According to this parable, the person who does not live their life with their whole heart is either thinking wrong or being lazy. God gave each of us the potential to fulfill a destiny.

At the end of my life, I hope to hear that I am a good and faithful servant, not a wicked and lazy person. I am working to invest everything I know and everything that I understand to help others achieve their destinies.

Conclusion

Cultivating my personal relationship with God.

Each day it is essential for me to hear from God as to what I should be doing and where I should be going. The blessing that He provides for me is on the path to the destiny He planned for me. If I come up with a good idea and ask Him to bless it, I could easily be on a road that would not lead me to my destiny. The person who made me and understands me is in the best position to show me what to do. I must understand how to initiate and cultivate a relationship with the One who can give me the best counsel because He knows me better than anyone else.

Throughout His Word, God provided many promises relating to healing, prosperity, and fullness of life to anyone who has a covenant relationship with Him. For example, Keith Moore listed promises in his book entitled "101 Healing Scriptures that Answer 'Is it God's Will to Heal?'" For many, these benefits God has provided are not realized.

Certain standards apply to life in general. God's commandments include concepts that will work for anyone who applies them, such as how personal hygiene contributes to health. The overall principle of reaping what a person sows in every area of life includes the keys to prosperity. These concepts will work regardless of the person's faith or commitment level because the outcome is based on laws God designed when the universe was created. The person who provides more value than he takes in business transactions will prosper over time, and that spiritual law is as certain as the physical law of gravity.

Many promises are conditional, based on our ability to keep our part of the covenant. God is righteous and cannot be intimate with unrighteousness, so an individual desiring to cultivate a personal relationship with God must be in right standing with Him. The portion of the scripture that does require a spiritual solution is the forgiveness for a person's wrongdoing. No one I know has been able to go through life without lying or without having a lustful thought. When you go back to the Basic Law as written in both the Tanakh and New Testament, I have never met anyone who has been able to keep the commandments perfectly. In the ancient Hebrew faith, the High Priest made atonement for sin annually. In the Christian world, Jesus became the perfected and sinless form of that sacrifice, which is why He was born of a virgin and gave His life. Our belief in Jesus is likened to Abraham's belief in God, which was imputed to him as righteousness long before the Law was given to Moses. Paul of Tarsus was an educated Pharisee in Jesus' day. He wrote many letters that were included in the New Testament of today. Paul said that to allow God to work in our individual lives, we must confess Jesus as our Lord and acknowledge that He was raised from the dead (Romans 10:9-10). Then we can approach God boldly because we have right-standing through the covenant that Jesus kept (Hebrews 4:14-

16). We are free to develop as close of a relationship with God as we want.

God communicates with us in multiple ways. He gave each of us a conscience, which is an internal mechanism to warn us before we make mistakes. In the Bible, He gave us scripture by His inspiration to guide us. This Word of God contains functional wisdom we can use in every situation we could ever encounter. As an example of the depth of God's understanding, Leviticus 14 outlines remedies for diseases in the time of Moses. Specific directions included putting healing oils on the right ear, the right thumb, and the right big toe. The person who inspired that writing displayed an understanding of the anatomy of the human body thousands of years ahead of medical experts on Earth.

God's Word provides principles. Scripture doesn't tell us who to marry or which job to take. The Bible tells us principles that we can apply to those decisions. As we study God's Word and develop a relationship with Him, we learn how to apply the passages. We can follow His direction that will bless us and get us to the destiny that God has designed for each of us. To receive specific information from God, a person must ask the Lord to be filled with the Holy Spirit. The Holy Spirit enters at the same moment an individual accepts what Jesus did as atonement for all wrong-doing, and a new spirit is created within the believer. Being filled allows the Holy

Spirit to communicate directly to each person through that born-again spirit.

In my case, the specific actions I needed to take to reverse the symptoms of the post-polio syndrome or rebuild muscles atrophied from the childhood virus were not detailed in God's Word. I needed to talk with God from my spirit. In the introduction, I explained that Wendy's face kept coming across my mind when I prayed. If I had used my mental capabilities only, I could have researched all types of rehabilitation for months. None of the information would have correlated the activities to polio. I would have still been confused. I probably spent a total of 10 minutes contemplating that I kept seeing Wendy's face in prayer before I called her.

Before Jesus ascended into heaven, He told his disciples not to leave Jerusalem until the Holy Spirit had come upon them. Having the fullness of the Holy Spirit must be important if Jesus said not to leave home without it. As we read the book of Acts, we see men standing in public before thousands of people, explaining that Jesus was the only way to have a right relationship with God. Less than two months earlier, these same men fled in fear at the mere thought others might associate them with Jesus. Peter, the lead spokesman, denied he even knew Jesus. Now that is an example of personal growth that cannot be accomplished naturally.

If you would like to discuss any questions you have about cultivating a deeper relationship with God, please contact Gary Keesee Ministries at 888-391-5433. Trained prayer ministers will answer your call 24 hours a day, seven days a week.

If you would like to reach me directly, please send a message to **dontgiveupriseupbook@gmail.com**.

Acknowledgments

I want to say thank you to the many people who have helped me become the person I am today. I am thankful for my parents, who demonstrated the compound effect long before Darren Hardy wrote about it. My parents would not accept the doctor's report that I could not walk normally after contracting polio. My Mom spent five hours a day exercising my leg until I could walk without a leg brace at six years old.

I am also thankful for the influence of my childhood pastors, Bill and Betty Jean Billingsley. During a church service when I was 10, I solemnly told God that I wanted to produce a 100-fold return in every area of my life.

More recently, multiple teachers on Kenneth Copeland's Victory channel enabled significant development in my life. In addition to Kenneth and his team teaching the basics of faith, Gary Keesee taught me how the kingdom of God worked. Andrew Wommack explained specifics about healing, and Bill Winston inspired me to be bold.

I owe the Yager mentoring group more than words can ever express through the associations and tools they have supplied. My direct mentors, Royal and Barbara Clevenger, have provided advice and direction in multiple areas of my life. I am able to associate with people who apply success concepts in a practical way through my mentoring group on Monday and Thursday evenings.

I am also thankful for my inner circle of friends who continue to encourage me through my journey.

Glenda Sentell Jordan

Glenda Sentell Jordan was brought up in a loving, Godly home. She contracted polio when she was six months old, which noticeably slowed down her physical development.

Although her childhood teachings focused on the blessing of eternal existence with God in heaven, Glenda always had a desire to see people live an abundant life in the here and now. After completing college, Glenda became a Certified Public Accountant. Early in her career, she earned a Master of Business Administration, as well as two other audit-related certifications. She later joined one of the world's largest telecommunications providers and eventually became a Director of the Internal Audit organization.

Over the years, her body experienced deterioration from the aftermath of the original polio infection. Fueled by her desire to see herself and others live the abundant life Jesus promised us, she began searching for ways to restore her body. Prior to leaving the corporate world, Glenda also joined a private mentoring group focused on assisting self-motivated individuals acquire cash flow assets.

Currently, Glenda is pursuing a black belt in martial arts and mentoring individuals who own independent businesses. She also owns her own business so she can share many of the health and wellness products that helped her on her journey with others.

Made in the USA
Columbia, SC
20 August 2024